COUNT THE CRITTERS

PIGLETS PLAYING: COUNTING FROM 11 TO 20

by Megan Atwood

illustrated by Sharon Holm

Content Consultant: Paula J. Maida, PhD

magic wagon

VISIT US AT
WWW.ABDOPUBLISHING.COM

Published by Magic Wagon, a division of the ABDO Group, PO Box 398166, Minneapolis, MN 55439. Copyright © 2012 by Abdo Consulting Group, Inc. International copyrights reserved in all countries. All rights reserved. No part of this book may be reproduced in any form without written permission from the publisher.

Looking Glass Library™ is a trademark and logo of Magic Wagon.

Printed in the United States of America, North Mankato, Minnesota.
102011
012012

♻ THIS BOOK CONTAINS AT LEAST 10% RECYCLED MATERIALS.

Text by Megan Atwood
Illustrations by Sharon Holm
Edited by Lisa Owings
Interior layout and design by Christa Schneider
Cover design by Christa Schneider

Library of Congress Cataloging-in-Publication Data

Atwood, Megan.
  Piglets playing : counting from 11 to 20 / by Megan Atwood ; illustrated by Sharon Lane Holm.
      p. cm. — (Count the critters)
  ISBN 978-1-61641-855-7
  1. Counting — Juvenile literature. I. Holm, Sharon Lane, ill. II. Title.
  QA113.A897 2012
  513.2'11 — dc23
                              2011033077

Counting is fun! Count from eleven to twenty as you watch these playful piglets run and romp in the barnyard.

Ten pink piglets play in the barnyard.

Mother Pig brings in spotted piglets.

Let's count all the new piglets!

One bounces ahead of the rest. She is
number eleven. Eleven comes after ten.

Piglets root and wrestle. One piglet sticks his nose in the dirt. He snorts and snorfles. He is number twelve. Count aloud: eleven, twelve.

17 18 19 20 11+1= 12

11 12 **13** 14 15 16

Piglets wrestle and root. One piglet wrestles with another piglet. She tumbles and trips and tramples. She is number thirteen. Count aloud: eleven, twelve, thirteen.

Piglets run and romp. One piglet chases another piglet along the fence. He runs fast! His little piglet ears blow back in the wind. He is number fourteen. Count aloud: eleven, twelve, thirteen, fourteen.

17   18   19   20   13+1= 14

Piglets romp and run. One piglet rolls in the mud. She splashes and squeals. This is her favorite way to cool off! She is number fifteen. Count aloud: eleven, twelve, thirteen, fourteen, fifteen.

17   18   19   20   14 + 1 = **15**

Piglets run and romp. One piglet hides
behind the barn. He is peeking out at you!

He is number sixteen. Count aloud: eleven, twelve, thirteen, fourteen, fifteen, sixteen.

17   18   19   20   15 + 1 = 16

Piglets slurp and snuggle. Mother Pig nurses her hungry piglets. They gulp and grunt. One piglet wants more milk. She is number seventeen. Count aloud: eleven, twelve, thirteen, fourteen, fifteen, sixteen, seventeen.

17 18 19 20 16+1= **17**

Piglets snuggle and slurp. One piglet has finished his meal. He is ready for a nap. He finds a good spot to drowse and dream. He is number eighteen.

Count aloud: eleven, twelve, thirteen, fourteen, fifteen, sixteen, seventeen, eighteen.

Piglets snooze and sleep. A bird sings the pile of piglets to sleep. One piglet lifts her head to listen to its lullaby. She is number nineteen.

Count aloud: eleven, twelve, thirteen, fourteen, fifteen, sixteen, seventeen, eighteen, nineteen.

17   18   **19**   20   18 + 1 = **19**

Piglets sleep and snooze. One last sleepy piglet joins the pile. We know there are ten pink piglets. Let's count the rest: eleven, twelve, thirteen, fourteen, fifteen, sixteen, seventeen, eighteen, nineteen, twenty! Sweet dreams, piglets!

17   18   19   **20**   19+1= **20**

Words to Know

bounce — to hit the ground and spring back up.

drowse — to fall into a light sleep.

nurse — how babies get milk from their mothers.

piglet — a baby pig.

romp — to run and play.

root — to poke and dig.

snooze — to take a nap.

trample — to crush by stepping hard on something.

tumble — to roll or fall.

wrestle — a contest where two individuals struggle to unbalance each other.

Web Sites

To learn more about counting from 11 to 20, visit ABDO Group online at **www.abdopublishing.com**. Web sites about counting are featured on our Book Links page. These links are routinely monitored and updated to provide the most current information available.